Old World Magick for the Modern World

Tips, Tricks, and Techniques to Balance, Empower, and Create a Life You Love

Patti Negri

Hollywood Psychic, Medium, "Good" Witch
pattinegri.com

Published by Efluential Publishing, LLC.

Photography by Gina Leslie (www.TheWellofImages.com)

Library of Congress Control Number: 2018968260

ISBN 978-1-7335455-0-1

For bulk purchases contact patti@pattinegri.com

CONTENTS

FOREWORD

ભૂ

Old World Magic for the Modern World by Patti Negri, is a simple, upbeat and refreshing guide to the practice of "Good" magic, incorporating the intrinsic, untapped and unique powers inside us all. This book is a compendium of practical spells and charms for everyday life drawn from many ancient religions, traditions and cultures. This enchanting little gem is short and sweet and is the perfect introduction to magic, as well an excellent resource to get just ideas flowing.

Old World Magic for the Modern World is just as useful for a beginner as it is for someone with knowledge of the subject. Patti guides readers through the feelings/thoughts people must harness in order for their worldly "intentions" or "desires" to manifest in combination with the performing of spells and rituals.

Patti's method shows people how to incorporate magic into their busy 21st century lives without adding any stress to their lives. Her preferred ingredients and tools are far from obscure and are easy to find; her spells incorporate everyday items found in kitchen cabinets together with few more unique items which can all be purchased very inexpensively on Amazon.com. The most powerful take-away for me stems from Patti's mantra, "magic is everywhere."

Every person's "internal magic" can be awakened and harnessed not only in order to boost spells and enhance rituals, but also to bring the "magic" in each person's imagination to life.

—Tania Bailey, Esq.

PATTI'S PATH

೧೧

In this book you will learn to bring **clarity, confidence, and courage** to your life with fun, simple, magickal practices.

Enlightenment is all about your relationship with yourself and with spirit. You will receive a collection of fun, easy, insightful techniques to open your awareness and your sight—and therefore your own self-empowerment! You will learn easy ways to truly take the driver's seat and be the architect of your life so you can create a life you truly love.

For the fulfillment of our heart's desires we need the willingness to step out of our cocoon of false beliefs and any limitations that appear to be sabotaging our efforts. The choice is ours, and it is greatly dependent upon how we view change: as an opportunity to release our fears and insecurities or as a challenge we prefer to avoid.

When the exploration of consciousness is interwoven with the unfolding of events in our everyday lives, we have made a conscious choice to discover and live our limitless potential. Our dreams really CAN come true! And it is as easy as we allow it to be—or as hard as we make it. Let's go for easy!

HOW I GOT HERE

☙☙

I was born in Southern California to a "typical middle class" American family. Third child, only girl, happy suburban home, with amazingly loving and supportive parents who stayed happily married forever. Life was truly good indeed. Picture perfect really . . . inside and out. But as far back as I can remember, I knew I was different; I knew that the "imaginary" creatures under the bed and in my room were not imaginary at all! I knew that they were real entities and beings that I could talk to, play with and get to know. I also knew that I was just not "overly sensitive," as my mom put it, when I would come home from school and tell her about what the other kids were thinking and saying about me. Again, this was just chalked up to my vivid imagination. I knew there was more to it. I became a seeker . . . even at a young age. I spent more time playing alone quietly in my room than anybody else I knew. And I actually had a wonderful, full world in my tiny pink suburban bedroom. I wrote poetry, played with my stuffed animals, Barbie dolls, and little rubber animals—and there was more. I traveled. Without leaving my room, I traveled near and far to see what was out there. I remember one time going with my mom to one of her friend's homes for a luncheon. I swore up and down that I had been there before. My mother assured me that I had not, that neither of us had been there before. Then I proceeded to tell her the color of every room within the house, right down to the pattern of the wallpaper in the bathroom, before we even entered the front door.

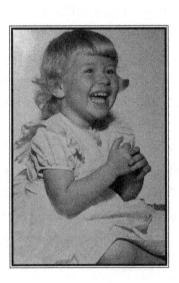

I was raised without any mention of God, religion, or family spiritual belief system. My mom had been loosely raised protestant and my father was raised by a "near evangelical" atheist—his famous psycho-analyst father Vitali Negri, who thought ANY spirituality, religion or non-scientific belief system was sheer ignorance. As I rode around in the back of my family car—as we passed churches, synagogues, and temples—I was envious of the people going in. I had never even uttered the word God before, think-ing it was almost some kind of naughty word. I knew these were places of mysticism and magick—and faith and belief in things that you can't see—but any more than that, I did not know, and for some reason was afraid to ask. I just had to find this mystical and spiritual "world beyond ours" on my own.

My obsession with "the beyond" grew and grew. I decided I needed to consciously contact a dead per-son. I was seven or eight years old. Unfortunately, I didn't really know any dead people, so I decided on Marilyn Monroe and John F. Kennedy, the two most famous deceased people I had heard of. I knew most of my "usual" contact with the other side was at night in the dark; since it was daytime, I went into our win-dowless hallway, closed all the doors, lined the cracks with towels, and dragged my best friend Sherry in with me. We sat cross-legged on the floor, and I started asking the spirits of Marilyn and JFK to enter the room. I asked, I pleaded, I believe I even created my first chant, and, lo and behold, the hallway filled with orbs of bright light. They started in the corner and quickly began filling the room. It was amazing. Sherry and I, being proper little girls, ran screaming out of the house; I had never been so excited. I had actually and consciously contacted the other side. My journey had begun.

In talking a bit more with my mom, I began to learn a little more about my family history—how her grandmother was clairvoyant and always knew when someone was going to die by an angel visiting her the night before. Even (years later) my mom was twice awakened in the middle of the night by a strange crackling sound in her ears that shot her straight up in bed. And on the other side of the world in Vietnam, my brother had just caught fire those same two times. So I figured it was genetic; I liked that. I also learned a bit about my father's side. My grandfather was of Turkish Sephardic heritage. Ahhhh—so I was a bit of Jewish gypsy. I liked that! More mysticism in my blood, whether acknowledged or not. This made sense; of course this is why I can talk to dead people and spirits. This new knowledge gave me great joy.

It wasn't until I was thirteen that I dared ask my parents if I could go to church. It was the "Jesus people" age of the seventies with some really fun stuff going on. So, with my heart pounding, I asked my mom, "Can I go to church with Sherry on Sunday? They are having a rock concert after the service."

To my surprise, she said, "Of course."

I thought, *Really? Really?* All these years of passing these magical places and I could've gone in anytime. Wow. Who knew! And so now my quest was again moving forward. I had discovered organized religion. I started with the fun hippie Jesus people (I can't tell you how many times I was baptized in the ocean by Pastor Chuck to the groovin' sounds of the latest Christian rock band).

And there was a reason for all my special insights and abilities . . . it was Jesus. Those spirits I used to communicate with were now angels sent from God. This revelation made me much less "weird" in my mind . . . just another wacky "Jesus freak." But even though I "felt the spirit," I knew something wasn't complete for me, that somehow this wasn't quite my right path.

It was fun being a "born again" for a few years. However, at age fifteen I learned I was DES exposed. Diethylstilbesterol was a drug my mom had taken when she was pregnant with me, prescribed by doctors and incorrectly believed to prevent miscarriages. This drug was now, as I reached young adulthood, making me very sick. Girls my age were dying from never-before-seen vaginal and cervical cancers; I was going through menopausal hot flashes instead of puberty. I had my first exploratory surgery at fifteen and was told I would never have children. I was devastated.

I certainly didn't know why my personal friend Jesus would let this happen to me or so many other innocent girls. I allowed myself to become a victim. I tried to keep my faith, but some of the fire had gone out. The Holy Spirit just wasn't as good or powerful as he used to be. I started shutting down some of my gifts and abilities and just focused on life on this human plane.

I had already been modeling locally a bit, so I took it up a notch, I got an agent and started being "the all-American teen" for TEEN Magazine and Kodak ads. It was fun. I didn't need spirituality; I had glossy spreadsheets and magazines with my face on them.

Though deep inside I knew that I still was not satisfied, I was still a seeker; I just preferred to do it in Hollywood instead of the "other world." I dated, I married, I divorced, I dated, I married, I divorced. Twice divorced at the ripe old age of twenty-five, I relocated to Hollywood to start over.

Life began again. This was the "new age" of the eighties. I loved it. Spiritual seekers were *en vogue* again, so I tried Judaism, Buddhism, Tibetan Buddhism and, of course, totally fell in love with Shirley MacLaine. I learned about crystals and chakras and connecting directly to spirit without need of an exact "guidebook" or religious leader. This was good. Very good. My special gifts and abilities were coming back. I started seeing auras again. Connecting to spirit, channeling—all the "cool stuff" of the eighties. I was so "out of my body" during parts of that time period that I literally had to wear a hat to keep from leaving my body. Thank goodness hats were popular!

But I still knew there was something more. This "new age" was all a little too "squeaky clean" for me. A little too orderly. I desired a spirituality that was earthier, grittier AND a bit more romantic. I started discovering the Shamanic and Earth Magic paths. I knew I liked working with elements and moon cycles, herbs and oils. The Native American path was close, but once I discovered the Pagan and Wiccan path, I knew it, or some form of it, would be the right one for me. It is empowering, fun and keeps that sense of magic and wonder I had as a child.

Though my path continues to change and grow—and, in all honesty, hard to put a real name on anymore—I have gone full circle back to practicing the same natural magick of my childhood. I have a life-affirming, earth and nature-oriented belief system that honors the natural world as the embodiment of divinity. My forte is in adjusting energy and flow in people, spaces, situations—most anything. I work organically by creating spells and rituals that arrange natural elements to the rhythms and cycles of the universe. This can help bring about healing, change our lives for the better, and create balance.

With my new path I was able to get my health back; not be a victim to a drug company's greed, dating back to when I was in my mother's womb, I have created a new healthy life for myself and continue to live into it every day. I love showing people how they can do the same. Magick is everywhere. Magick is at our fingertips. Magick works. (Adding the "k" on the end of magic is meant to differentiate it from the card-trick kind!)

For years I kept my worlds very separate. I had my own beautiful spirituality, a small support group of the most amazing like-minded women, and to the public lived the typical life of a hopeful Hollywood actress—with my value and worth determined daily by my achievements and failures in varying degrees. I knew I needed more challenge, and more control over my career, so I established a production company and began producing live shows. With my improv and sketch background, combined with my film and TV experience, I created a fun and creative little niche for myself in the corporate show market. I certainly used my spiritual gifts in my work, but nobody knew it. People just thought I was "insight-ful" or had "good intuition" ;o) Life was good again.

Then the recession hit and corporate entertainment became a dirty word. Companies could not hire big, fun musical shows for their employees while simul-taneously laying them off (even if they were teaching them team-building skills and motivation). The bottom fell out of my company. I still had kept one foot in the film and TV world and was really liking this new "reality" genre—not the big "sensationalist" stuff, but the good, fun, unpredictable storytelling that reminded me of my improv days. I did a couple shows and became known to the reality world as my actor/producer self.

Then, someone who knew me as a witch, and knew my work doing séances and house blessings, asked me to do their show as that spiritual persona of myself. *Hmmm*, I thought. *That would definitely take me "out of the broom closet."* And I wondered if it would hurt my standing in the corporate world. Would Microsoft really want some witch doing a murder mystery for the staff of their accounting department? Then it hit me . . . it didn't matter! THIS was part of my path. It was coming together. Combining my whole life, all the separate components, into one complete package. This silly, fabulous, TV platform is just one area where I can share my gifts and my message of hope and possibility. So I jumped in with both feet—and, surprisingly, Microsoft DID hire a witch to do a murder mystery for their accounting department. I have yet to be burned at the stake, and I am honored to be given the opportunity to show "my kind" as loving, positive, spiritual people with a message of love, hope, and magick!

I am proud to be an actor, producer, psychic medium, civic activist, and practicing white witch. Yes, I proudly admit that I have been able to communicate with the spirit world since I was a toddler and conducted my first séance at the age of seven or eight. I am thrilled to have conducted séances on radio, film, TV, and in living rooms and board rooms across America.

The chief lesson so far on my journey is that life is what we make it. Yes, we are given a set of circumstances, some good, some not-so-good, some possibly horrible. But I believe we are in charge of what we do with them, where we go from there. I choose a life of hope, of possibility, of love. I believe that magick is all around us in many forms and many names. I believe that we can connect into that magickal energy and use and harness it to have a better, fuller, happier life. I believe that spirit is all around us—and is truly there to help us if we only are aware of and acknowledge it.

My deepest sadness is how "asleep" so many people seem to be to the magick and wonder around them. They go through life boxed in by their own limitations, versus the limitlessness of possibility. My sincerest hope is for those people to wake up to the wonder, to take charge of their lives and find the magick within. If I can help in the tiniest of ways, I will consider my journey successful.

WHAT IS PRACTICAL MAGICK?

Practical Magick is simple techniques, spells, and thought patterns that everyone can do to improve their day-to-day life and help them live a magickal life every day!

You don't have to be a witch or psychic!

Everything is a combination of Mind, Body, and Spirit to create the shift, open the door, enhance the opportunity. Practical Magick will provide you with a new perception to move forward in the direction you want with a bit more grace, ease, and enjoyment as you manifest the life you want! Within these pages you will learn everything from how to deal with difficult relationships, your own personal blocks, fears and limitations, to how to develop your own psychic ability and intuition and tune into your own guides and deity. **Who has the power? YOU do!** (If not, who or what have you given it away to?) I will teach you how to be the master of your universe; the architect of your own life.

MIND, BODY, SPIRIT
CONNECTION

The one thing we know from the 200,000 books written about it is that everything we do must include mind, body, and spirit. One out of three is "wishful thinking." Two out of three is "hit or miss" at best. Three out of three is a "home run!" Breaking it down, before we do anything, we must first envision that action in our head; in our thought process. We don't do ANYTHING without it being a thought first. Examples: "I'm going to be rich," "I'm going to eat," "I am going bowling," "Everybody takes advantage of me," etc. Then our bodies act after the thought. We start the process of making money, eating, bowling—or even the manifestation of people taking advantage of us. (People most always DO live up to our expectations . . . keep aware of that!) The third and often elusive is the "spirit" element. It's less tangible; harder to grasp. But, the spirit aspect is the "battery power" that makes it happen. It's like the aspirin for the headache. Spirit can be created a lot of ways: via prayer or affirmations, vision boards, spells, and magickal workings, or it can be done via the elements. Every element has some specific attributes. You will be using all of these techniques, elements, and spells through living your belief system.

To me it is all about Awareness—Awareness, Intent, and Conscious Creation. Let's live our lives "awake," which is very different from living on "auto pilot," "phoned in," or "asleep at the wheel." This book is the perfect place to get started. We know that where you put your energy is where you live. Start putting your energy into the things you want—not the things you don't have. The classic "glass half empty versus glass half full" is a perfect place to start. Yes, fate exists, but free will and manifestation outweigh it by a landslide. Begin creating a life you love. While you can't control everything around you, you CAN control how you react to the things around you—and that changes EVERYTHING!

ELEMENTAL BALANCING EXERCISES

✆

Or What I Like to Call
30 Seconds to Fix Anything!

I think the key to almost everything is balance. Every once in a while (well heck almost daily) we get or feel a little out of balance. Here are my super easy elemental exercises to help get you back in balance within thirty seconds almost anywhere you are!

Picture your entire life in the four basic elements. Earth. Air. Fire. Water. Your Earth is who you are, your home, your sense of being, the womb. Your Air is your thinking brain, your thoughts, your sense of reason (and often that chatter that won't shut up when you want it to). Your Fire is your passion, creativity, the blood in your veins, your spirituality. Your Water is your emotions . . . and remember water is about 60 percent of our body and 70 percent of our planet, so our emotions are a big part of who we are. So, the next time you are not as happy as you can be, or productive as you can be, or even as awake and conscious as you would like to be, you have a choice. Instead of just staying in that state, decide which of those four elements is the most out of balance. I promise, one of them will be!

Water/Emotions . . . Is it your emotions that are out of balance? Are you angry or sad or worried about something? Whether held inside or screamed out the window, whether justified or not, if it is your emotions keeping you from your full experience of life in this moment, you need the water element. An attribute of water is emotion. Think of it like an aspirin for a headache. Just think how good you feel after a shower. It's the water! You can't jump in a shower every time you're sad or angry or worried, but you can almost always find running water. A sink, a kitchen, a bathroom, a drinking fountain or a hose. So, going back to the mind, body, and spirit equal "home run" formula, walk up to that sink and turn on the water. First, set your intent (mind) and perhaps tell your higher self, God, or your spirit guides that with this water you are releasing the extra emotion. Then run your hands under the water for thirty seconds (body or action). If you want, you can visualize that anger or sadness running down the drain. The water itself is the "spirit" or battery power! You now have all three elements, so within thirty seconds you will have healthfully released that excess emotion. Gone. Not stuffed down or ignored or discounted—just gone. If you need to deal with what caused the emotion, you can now do it without the overwhelm of it. Give it a try—I think you will be pleasantly amazed!

Air/Thoughts . . . Do your thoughts get the best of you sometimes? Do you overthink? Get foggy? Sometimes can you just not get your thoughts to SHUT UP? If so, you need the air element.

An attribute of air is thought. In these rushed modern times, very few of us breathe deeply. Unfortunately, the effect of shallow, quick breathing goes directly to your head! Just being aware of your breathing can be a huge help in itself, but my "magick fix" for foggy brain is adding some sound to your breath—vowel sounds to be exact. Any vowel, any order. Vowels literally clear the head. Think about how almost every sacred word or chant is a vowel—"amen," "om," etc.

So next time you get chatty or foggy brain, do my one, two, three (mind, body, spirit) quick fix. First set your intention that with your deep slow breathing and vowel sounds you will clear and quiet your mind . . . then just DO IT! Within thirty seconds, you will actually notice the chatter in your head begin to stop—and the fog clear up. This is great to do before a presentation or important conversation—or anytime you need clear thinking!

Earth/Grounding . . . If you are not feeling "grounded" or "in your body," you need to tap into the earth element. It's great to get outside in nature. Get barefoot in the dirt or grass. Hug a tree—literally! However, if you are on the thirty-fifth floor of an office building going into a very important meeting and feeling a little "queasy," grab ANYTHING that is wood or stone—a pencil, a wooden chair, or desk, the granite countertop, a crystal, even the diamond, opal, or any stone in your ring. Grab onto it. Decide in your head that this item will ground and center you. Hold on to the object. Deep breathe for thirty seconds. Everyone feels this one a little differently. I feel like a warm earthen blanket surrounds me. Some people feel like "roots' are coming out of the soles of their feet into the ground. However you experience this, you WILL feel immediately grounded and centered.

Fire/Passion . . . If you are feeling tired, passionless, or not inspired, you need to call in the fire element. Maybe you have a hot date with your honey and just not "feeling it." Or perhaps you are working on a creative or art project and need inspiration; maybe you are just exhausted, in bed, and have to get up! You have all the "earth" you need, but you need the "fire" power to rise and shine.

This, like air, is breathing and sound magick. First, set in your mind what you want, as you did with the other elements, then do thirty seconds of deep breathing while going zzzzzzzzzzzzzzzz. (Ask any eight-year-old what sound a bee makes . . . you've got it!) Within thirty seconds, you will start to feel a tingling in the base of your spine. It will rise up and in no time at all you will have all the energy, passion, and creativity you need to move forward.

These four techniques really can be like your hidden superhero powers! You can do them anywhere. They cost nothing and take only thirty seconds. Keep them in your invisible back pocket—and pull them out whenever needed for immediate balance and relief!

BASIC SPELL CASTING

As we get into some of the more magickal sections of this book, I want to give you some basics. I personally do not believe that you must be a witch or a psychic to do spell work and magick. But there are definitely some rules and guidelines you should follow. The power that makes a spell work is not to be found in a book. The real power that makes a spell work lives within you and the energy around you.

The secret of successful spell casting, as with all magick, is your intent, your belief, and your connection to divinity. Your thoughts, willpower, feelings, and physical exertions are actually all expressions or forms of this divine energy. When you understand the true nature of the energy you work with, you can make real magick.

There are no hard and fast rules of how to cast a spell, but there are some basic elements. Implement them in a way that feels right to you.

1. Create or cast a sacred space (light candles, incense, or whatever feels right).
2. Call upon divinity (however YOU see it: God, higher self, universe, your guides, whatever!)
3. State the goal of your spell.
4. Visualize your goal.
5. Raise energy by chanting, dancing, or drumming.
6. Direct your energy to the spell's goal.
7. Release the energy of your spell, ground any excess energy.
8. Offer thanks and close your circle.
9. Act in accord and give back in thanks.

Tips for Successful Spell Casting:

- Passion fuels a successful spell; doubt can kill it.
- Have a clear goal.
- Rhyming is great! An old adage says that spells should rhyme. A rhymed spell has rhythm and joyfulness in it, it's easy to remember and repeat, and the repetition itself creates an altered, magickal consciousness.

There are many ways/methods to work. I usually work elementally, which is based on an elemental compass. Most Wiccans, Native Americans, and Shamanic beliefs work elementally. I like it because it is just working with our natural earth energy and does not conflict with religious or spiritual belief systems!

So, working an elemental compass, here are the properties and directions of the elements:

East/Air: intelligence, organization, thoughts, clarity

South/Fire: warmth, passion, change

West/Water: emotions, love, contentment, unity, purification

North/Earth: stability, strength, nurturing, home, womb

A spell is only used to control yourself, never another or nature. Do not do spell work on someone else's behalf without his or her permission. Before performing your spell, carefully think through all the possible repercussions to make certain that it does not have a manipulative component, which means doing ANYTHING to ANYONE without his or her permission.

Say you want love, for example. Do a love spell to "bring the perfect love into your life." That is GOOD magick. Do NOT do a love spell on a specific person. No matter how sweet or harmless that seems, unless you have that person's permission, that is black magick and manipulative—and guaranteed to go wrong for all parties. No matter how you may be tempted, DON'T DO IT! The "'karmic cost" is way too high. Spells should not be entered into lightly without thoroughly considering all of the possible effects. There is also a simple "keep you out of trouble" rule: "An' it harm none, do what thou wilt," meaning "do whatever you wish as long as it harms no one." Follow those guidelines, then go out and create some magick. Always stay in integrity. Always work in the "light," and all will be well!

MOON MAGICK

Bring a Little into Your Life

We make New Year's resolutions . . . we keep some of them, and others we don't—and life goes on either way. Often, we find ourselves in a bit of a rut where each day runs into the next without much delineation. Here is one simple, fun, and powerful way to change that—follow the moon!

As stated in the elemental balancing exercises earlier, we are almost 70 percent water. Just like the moon affects the tides, we are affected the same way. It's not just the "full moon" that makes everybody crazy . . . we are subtly affected by ALL the moon cycles. If we tap into these cycles, we can shift the things we want in our lives a whole lot faster, with grace and ease, by just tuning into them.

Without getting into anything complicated, here's how you can easily add a little moon magick into your life. The basics: We have a full moon about once a month. In the two weeks leading up to a full moon, the moon is waxing (getting bigger); in the two weeks after a full moon, the moon is waning (getting smaller). The perfect time to "add things" into your life is while the moon is getting bigger, transitioning from new moon to full moon. A little more love, a little more fun, a little more laughter or money, or all of the above.

Conversely, the perfect time to "let go" of things you no longer want or need is after the full moon, when it is getting smaller or waning. This is a great time to quit smoking, lose a couple pounds, clean out that closet, stop being hard on yourself, etc. During the dark or new moon, it's a great time to look inward a bit; during the full moon it's a great time to celebrate, give thanks, do magick, dance and create.

Even if just for a few minutes a day, be aware of the moon's cycle and "act accordingly"; you can get a lot accomplished and add texture, productivity, and joy to your life. Instead of watching month after month slip by, you now have this beautiful texture, like breathing or a tide, where you have two weeks of manifesting and two weeks of clearing.

Make a point of actually going outside and looking at the moon. Do it often. You will be amazed, and you've nothing to lose. It's fast, it's fun, it's free—and you will notice positive changes almost immediately. Use the same "adding during waxing" and "releasing during waning" to your spell working as well!

LOVE MAGICK

☙☙

It's All About Love . . .

Whether you are looking for love, or wanting to bring a little fire back into the love you have, here are a few of my fun, simple "magick" tips on how to bring more love into your life.

Love is love, romance starts with YOU! Date nights, romantic dinners, fresh flowers, sexy bubble baths, candles . . . you've got to get comfy with it! Even if you are by yourself, bring romance into your life, and soon a partner will follow. Make sure there is room in your heart AND in your home for love! Is there room in your closets and drawers for someone else? Is your bedroom "ready" to bring someone home to, just in case?

These simple things can help bring that love to you—and it certainly lets the universe know you are now ready for love. If you are already in a relationship, the theory is the same: Be the love you want to have and your partner will follow. Surprise your lover every once in a while with the unexpected, something you would like him or her to do for you, something he or she will certainly appreciate as well. It just takes one person to start a lovefest!

Love in the Kitchen

- Never cut parsley; it is bad for love (tear it instead).
- Eating together is bonding.
- Stir clockwise and add "love" with every turn.
- Stir counterclockwise to remove any anger or bad feelings.
- Put love and intention in everything you make.
- Apples really are a love fruit. (Slice of apple pie, anyone?)
- Tomatoes are good for prosperity, protection, and love.
- Anything red is primal and adds passion.
- Basil causes sympathy. Add a little basil to your food after a fight.
- Roses, lavender, and cinnamon all enhance and bring love.

Friday is the day of Venus, the Goddess of Love.

Add some extra "oomph" to any love spell or potion's potency by doing it on a Friday. A little planning ahead can bring you extra luck in love. Just remember to NEVER do a love spell on a specific person!

Catnip Attraction Spell

This is extremely easy to do and can quickly attract a new love interest into your life. Soak catnip in cinnamon water overnight. (Use purified water, and sprinkle cinnamon into it.) Strain the liquid and sprinkle it on your doorstep every evening for twenty-one days in the shape of a new crescent moon.

Love Potion Tea

Combine a pinch of rosemary, three mint leaves, and six rose petals. Boil three cups of water, then steep the combined dry ingredients. Once steeped, add nine drops of vanilla extract. Sip to bring in love!

Remember to **VISUALIZE** that love as you drink it! Brew on a Friday for extra "oomph."

HOME & SPACE
CLEARING MAGICK

৩১০

Clearing, Blessing, Cleansing Your Home, Office and Business

We all feel better in a "clean" home. Energetic cleansing is just as important as the dust, mop, and broom kind! Here are some easy ritual ideas for a house blessing or clearing. This can also be done in your office or workspace.

It's not just "haunted" houses that need clearing. If you are noticing negative energies or feelings in your home—perhaps unexplained tiredness, conflict, a restless, listless or "down" feeling—it is probably time to do a house clearing! Oftentimes, dark or negative energies or spirits gather like dust bunnies and can heavily affect the people living within.

House blessings are highly recommended for moving into a new home or apartment, after a divorce, death, or break up, or after any life- or situation-changing moments. Sometimes you just need to get the "stale" out and start off on a clean slate by removing old or negative energy from the home—kind of like a "spring cleaning"—in ANY season!

If you're moving into a new home and wish to bring in as much harmony as possible, it is smart to perform some type of cleansing and blessing on your new residence. Locations can hold the energy of previous owners or events that have happened there, and it is unlikely that it is all positive and loving. Don't take chances. While moving time is often stressful and busy, try to set one day aside to spiritually prepare your new home.

A house cleansing should be a celebration, so if you want, you can invite your friends and family and ask them to participate in blessing your home.

Use the following as a guideline. Feel free to adjust or make your own as spirit leads you.

Here are some simple and easy to get supplies you can use:

- A broom
- Sage or Palo Santo for clearing
- A white candle
- A sweet or sacred incense (Frankincense, Myrrh, Sandalwood, anything angelic, etc.)
- A bell or chime

If you feel negative spirits or dark energy, also get some Cascarilla powder (ground egg shells). You can buy it online or at a metaphysical or spiritual store.

First, walk through the space. Whether you have lived there twenty years or are just moving in, see if you can "feel or sense" dark or stuck areas. Notice how you feel in each area of the home. This is to get a lay of the land and to really notice the big difference after the clearing.

Go to the "heart" of the house to set up your sacred area. Often, this is the kitchen or dining room table or the coffee table in the living room or den. (A table is helpful to set up your supplies; you can always set them up on the floor if needed.)

Lay out your supplies. Create a sacred space in your own manner.

Light your candle. Light the incense. Set your intention to clear and clean your space of all bad energy and negativity. You can do a prayer or call in your deity, guides, elements, etc.

The ritual will be done in two sessions. First the clearing (done counterclockwise through the space) and then the blessing or filling (done clockwise through the space).

To clear, take your broom and literally "sweep" the bad energy out of each space and area (including corners and ceilings). You don't have to literally "touch" the areas with your broom bristles if you are afraid of scratching surfaces, but you can! Also, take the sage or Palo Santo room to room to further clear. You can do these one at a time or, if there is a group of you doing it, do it together, each taking one aspect. If you want more jobs for more people, add someone playing a hand drum, bell, or "clapping" the negativity out with their hands. Get creative. There is no right or wrong way to do it. Someone can sprinkle Cascarilla powder at doorways, windows, and thresholds if needed/desired. Just keep all your focus on clearing, cleaning, releasing, and removing. Go counterclockwise through the rooms and house as much as you can. Have fun with it, but also take it seriously! The house should feel really good after this—open and clean. A lot of people stop here, but I believe we are only halfway done. Once you have a clean space, you now have to fill it with all the good things you want!

Now, go room to room clockwise (opposite of how you did it before) to replenish the space with good, loving, positive, light, and energy. Take the candle room to room to bring in light. Carry the sweet incense into each room. Ring the chime in every room—each item bringing its own element and energy. This time, while in each room, claim and state the intentions and attributes you want in that room. For example, while standing at the front door, state who is allowed in! "The only people allowed in are people invited in, people with respect for you and your home, etc." In the kitchen you may ask for sustenance, nutrition, yummy food, and full cupboards. Love, sleep, rest, and great sex in the bedroom. Good friends, conversation, and laughter in the dining room. Cleanliness, good elimination, beauty, and good self-image in the bathroom. Etcetera, etcetera. Each room will fill up with all the emotions and attributes you put into it. Plus, there will be no room for the bad energies to get back in! You will feel the subtle difference in every space. Again, give your 100 percent commitment to your intentions, and have lots of fun with the process. Gather round at the starting point. Give thanks and enjoy your shiny new home!

DREAM MAGICK

ᴏᴥᴏ

Well, "Dream School" is what I call it! Night-time is a wonderful time to connect to spirit and get answers and guidance from the universe. Plus, dream school is a wonderful tool in developing one's own intuition and psychic ability! One reason is that it gives us the opportunity to get our logical brain out of the way for a while. Many tend to overthink things, and sometimes that is not the most advantageous mindset for spiritual growth and enlightenment. Let's explore a simple technique anyone can use.

Part One of Dream School: Glass of Water
First, set a glass of water by your bed at night. Water is an amazing "dream enhancer." Plus, as an added bonus, a glass of water by the bed actually collects any negative energies that may come in during the

night, so you are getting two benefits from one simple glass of water!

*(Please note: you should never drink the water right by
your bed because it has spent the night gathering up
and collecting these energies. Ever notice how bedside
water just doesn't taste very good in the morning? That
is why! Use it to water plants if you want, but keep your
drinking water farther away than your bedside table.)*

Okay, back to Dream School. You have your glass of
water by the bed. As you lay down, ask your guides or
higher power (or whatever you believe in) to come to
you in your dreams to help you with any guidance or
questions you may have. Or just let them know you

are "enrolling in Dream School" and want to develop and learn in your sleep. Then just go to sleep! At first you may or may not remember your dreams— or they may not make sense—but in time, you will notice a new, clear direction or path or understanding is unfolding. It will get clearer and clearer, and you can ask for any specifics as it develops.

Part Two of Dream School: Morning

If you have a set time you have to get up, set your alarm for ten minutes before that. When your alarm rings, again ask for guidance from the divine in your life path, or just in your day ahead, then hit the "snooze" button and know you have ten minutes to travel to the world between awake and sleep for some final "schooling." This is a perfect time when you are sleepy and not focused on your left and rational brain. When you wake up at the next alarm, you will feel a slight sense of direction, clarity, and focus to start your day!

Part Three of Dream School: Power Space

When you first get up, take a few minutes to think about anything you may have received. Think about how you feel and any thoughts going through your head. Don't sensor yourself—just let the thoughts flow! Again, with just a little practice, new information and insights will come flooding in every morning!

I recommend setting up a little altar or "power space" next to your bed. It doesn't have to be religious or spiritual, though it certainly can be.

Put a few things there that empower you: a photo, a candle, a flower. Perhaps a crystal, statue, or rock you found along a path—things that help you feel good about YOU! Keep a pad of paper or journal there. Allow yourself at least three minutes every morning to journal your new, expanding thoughts and understanding. Perhaps get some crayons or colored pencils to draw what you see or feel if you don't feel like writing. Either way, you are literally helping develop your intuition and psychic ability with every word or color stroke. Don't worry if you don't know what to write or draw at first—just let it flow. No one ever has to see it. You will be surprised at how, in just a short time, more messages and clarity are going to come out of your writings or drawings—or even from your Crayola color choices! Plus, it is just plain fun and helps develop your creativity as well as your intuition. With only a few extra minutes every day, you can expand your universe by galaxies.

Give it a try! I promise, it will open up a whole new magickal world for you. Remember, magick is EVERYWHERE!

BATHROOM MAGICK

ex/o

There are so many ways to incorporate bathrooms into your daily magick. Your bathroom functions can easily become magickal rituals that help you relax, invigorate, focus, manifest, and empower—all while doing your daily routine! One of my favorites is a "white bath." I put in a little salt for cleansing, sugar for sweetness, and milk for nurturing. You will feel a little like you are breakfast cereal, but you can rinse off afterwards and the benefits are amazing! A simple grounding and detoxing bath is Epsom salts and baking soda, or try some rose petals and rose quartz for a self-love ritual.

If you don't have a bath tub, you can get the same effect with just a foot bath! Or you can use a shower and put any herbs and salts wrapped in a cloth bag.

Even a pinch of salt thrown on the floor of your quickie shower can turn it into a cleansing shower!

I like to carve sigils (inscribed or painted symbols considered to have magickal power) on soap to manifest things. Looking for love? Carve a heart in your soap. Money? Carve a dollar sign! If you use liquid soap, draw or write on the bottle of your soap with a permanent marker. You can do the same with your shampoo and conditioner. So the daily act of cleansing now becomes ritual magickal manifestation!

Even when the soap wears down, or marker wears off, your soap has been empowered with your intent! You can also use sigils on soap when you want to banish something from your life. As the soap dissolves when

you're washing up, imagine your troubles dissolving with it.

You can enchant your toothbrush and toothpaste to make your speech more eloquent and charming. Spearmint is said to give you these qualities, and it is easy to find spearmint toothpaste!

The toilet can be used to literally flush your troubles away. All your lower chakras are open when you are going to the bathroom. Just a pinch of salt in the commode before you sit down can turn your toilet into a magickal water cauldron where you literally flush away your worries, anger, or fear with your normal body waste elimination! Mirrors are extremely powerful tools, especially in glamour magick. Empower  your mirror to reflect good health, good body image, and self-love. The most mundane of daily activities can turn into powerful, magickal rituals to bring magick into your life every day!

MY FAVORITE PROTECTION ITEMS, TOOLS AND TECHNIQUES

ॐ

Not everyone has a magickal pair of ruby slip-pers; just the regular day-to-day actions of life can sometimes leave us a bit vulnerable. I am talking energetically here. Whether it's spirits from beyond, or just a bundle of negativity from a person, group or space, here are a few of my favorite protection techniques!

My number one technique is intent—YOUR intent! Whether on a paranormal investigation or sitting with your in-laws, your awareness and intent is the strongest tool you have. You can honestly choose not to be negatively affected by someone who is throw-ing bad energy at you (whether purposely or not). With living folks, surround yourself with mirror energy.

Visualize your whole body being protected by a big mirrored egg.

Empower the egg so that nothing negative can get through it. You can visualize other materials as well (steel, titanium, iron), but with mirror, the added benefit is that the people throwing shade at you (especially if they are doing it on purpose) will actually get a bit of a "reflection" in your mirror and see how unattractive they look doing it. The mirror will also "bounce" the energy right back at them, so they will get a tiny taste of their own medicine. The best part is that you don't have to change your way of being. You can just stay safe and happy and smiling in your protective egg, and they will see through it enough to notice you are not being affected by their energy, therefore not getting the payoff they wanted. So the next time they just won't try so hard until it stops altogether! It sounds a little nuts, I know, but try it—it works!

You can even practice in an elevator or crowded space where no one is sending you bad energy. You can put up your mirror and actually see the people around you step back a bit, and usually smile (since they are not sending you bad energy). If it is so crowded they can't step back, you will notice that no matter how tight, your "personal space" will no longer feel invaded! Give it a try. Let me know what you think. Now back to the "spirit" realm.

I believe 100 percent that this three-dimensional world of ours is OUR realm of existence. Spirits on

the other side have to play by our rules unless we give them power over us (often just by not knowing better). So if a spirit, presence, or energy comes into a room that feels negative—or you just don't want it—command it to leave!

Use the name of whatever you believe in, the name of God or your angels or your own power. You will be amazed by the power you have. Do not do it with anger or fear, as that will feed a negative spirit. Just do it like a disciplinarian parent talking to their child. About 99.9 percent of the time, that spirit will leave. As far as protective items for your body and home, I love sigils and symbols. The Norwegian Helm of Awe is one of my favorites, as it just breaks apart negative energy into bits.

HELM OF AWE SIGIL

Most importantly, use something that works with YOUR belief system!

For clearing spaces, I love Cascarilla powder.

It's inexpensive, nontoxic (pure eggshells), and super protective for you home. Sprinkle it on windowsills, thresholds, and other areas to get rid of stagnations, or stir into your bath to clear your aura.

I also love Palo Santo wood, which is super clearing and protective, and not as harsh as sage.

PALO SANTO WOOD

I could write a whole book on this stuff—oh wait, I AM!

KITCHEN MAGICK

Okay, I am going to start this off by admitting I am really NOT a cook! (Those of you who know me, know that very well.)

Yes, I did beat 70,000 people for a spot on Master Chef a couple years ago. Yes, I DID win "Betty Crocker Future Homemaker of America" for my high school several decades back, but those are due to my manifesting and magickal abilities, truly NOT my cooking skills.

You do not have to be a good cook to bring magick into your kitchen. Even a bowl of instant oatmeal or frozen dinner CAN be imbued with real magick. We have to eat to survive. Why not use this daily function as a method for working magick? Actually, many people, regardless of their belief system, use magickal cooking. How many mothers feed their children tomato soup and grilled cheese sandwiches (both foods have healing correspondences) when they are home sick from school? How often have you indulged in some chocolate ice cream (for love and lifting spirits) to boost your mood after a fight with a loved one? The foods themselves correspond to the intent in both of these scenarios, and these examples are actually using magickal cooking!

I believe all objects can contain power and magick. Eggs symbolize fertility in spring, dried orange slices are reminders of the sun in mid-winter to align our bodies, spirits, and senses to the pace and mood of the Earth's changes.

You can prepare the following foods to help increase and amplify "psychic awareness": Bay, Celery, Cinnamon, Dandelion, Lemongrass, Mace, Nutmeg, Rose, Thyme, Bamboo Shoots, Celery, Mushrooms, Soy Bean Sprouts, Coconut, Dandelion Coffee, Fish, Fresh Flowers, Fresh Juices, Mulberry, Peppermint Tea, Shellfish, Soups of all Kinds (except potato), Sprouted Bread, Sushi, Tofu, Vegetable Soup

To increase and amplify "protection," prepare the following foods: Cabbage, Bell Pepper, Onion,

Radish, Basil, Horseradish, Mustard, Paprika, Clove, Cayenne, Fennel, Garlic, Rosemary, Artichoke, Kohlrabi, Brussels Sprouts.

Love in the Kitchen: Never cut parsley; it is bad for love. Eating together is bonding. Stir clockwise. Put love and intention in everything you make.

"Love" food: Apples, two people eat, they will fall in love! Tomatoes are good for prosperity, protection, love. Red is primal. Basil causes sympathy; it is a good appetizer and good if you are in an argument. Cinnamon is great for love and passion. Brazil nuts, apricots and Venus-inspired foods represent love, lust and beauty.

Before you begin cooking, hold the ingredients you are going to use and visualize your goal, charging it with your energies. As you prepare the food, keep this intent in mind. Stir clockwise to add positive energy and intent into your food. Stir counter-clockwise to remove negativity, stress, or anger. Even your morning cup of coffee can become a magickal elixir with the right intent! Remember, magick is EVERY-WHERE . . . especially in your kitchen!

BODY AND WEIGHT
LOSS MAGICK

༺❧༻

Wanna lose a little?
It's fun, easy, and effective!

If you are like me, sometimes we gain a few extra pounds during the holiday and winter months. And, as the weather starts to warm, we shed our big coats and want to shed some of those extra pounds as well.

Weight has always been an issue of mine, so the mere fact I have been on a diet most of my life; I consider myself an expert, so I decided to share some of my favorite and most effective techniques for losing those pounds using real magick. Yes, of course, diet and exercise are the most important parts, but here are some of my tried and true magickal techniques that can help you along your way!

Spend a moment or two thinking about the things that keep you from losing the excess weight. Write out everything you are truly ready to let go of. Write how much weight you want to lose and what bad habits you are willing to release. Now concentrate on all the negative aspects of dieting (cravings, temptations, cheating, hard work). Write all these things down on a piece of paper and really put your passion into it. See, smell, feel these things you're writing down and are READY TO LET GO OF!

Then, in a fire-safe bowl, burn the paper while chanting, "BURN, BURN, BURN AWAY. BURN THESE STUBBORN POUNDS TODAY." Keep chanting while it burns. Put every bit of belief and desire into releasing these things getting in your way. You should feel literally "tired and relieved" by the time the paper is gone (and really ready for some positive results)!

Now we are going to do some cord and knot magick, so you can catch and contain the magick as well!

Cut a string or cord to approximately the size of your waist. Then, one at a time, tie nine evenly spaced knots in the cord (blowing on and breathing life

into each knot with your breath as you pull the knot tight), saying with each:

First knot: "By knot of one, I now ignite a reduction in my appetite."

Second knot: "By knot of two, my metabolism becomes an active mechanism."

Third knot: "By knot of three, I bind desire for unhealthy foods; it now expires."

Fourth knot: "By knot of four, I bind the urge to binge and gobble, gorge and splurge."

Fifth knot: "By knot of five, inertia goes and exercise, I don't oppose."

Sixth knot: "By knot of six, all excess weight is released to quickly dissipate."

Seventh knot: "By knot of seven, I resist servings larger than two fists."

Eighth knot: "By knot of eight, insecurity goes, self-worth buds and blooms and grows."

Ninth knot: "By knot of nine, I bind setbacks, so I can easily stay on track."

Then close your eyes and visualize the image of you slowly shrinking in size, till you get to that desired weight and appearance. Keep the string close to you while you lose your weight. You can wear it around your wrist or neck or keep it tucked in your bra or pocket.

Here comes the real powerful EVERYDAY magick! Do the following until you reach your desired weight . . .

Any time before you eat, light a candle to Venus while you dine, even little snacks!

Let the power of Venus transform your whole eating experience. Before you eat, say to yourself, "I **am beautiful, I am strong, Let this spell make me well.**" When you're done, leave a small morsel as a token offering. Burn the candle whenever you eat, and at least fifteen minutes daily, and snuff (don't blow) out the candle. When you are in a place where you cannot light a candle, imagine one so strongly in your mind that you can nearly see it right there on the table in front of you.

Get two jars and some marbles or stones (enough marbles for each pound you want to lose). Display them where you will see them every day. (Kitchen is a good spot!) On one jar write, "TO LOSE," on the other write, "LOST." For every pound you lose, move a marble from the "to lose" to the "lost" jar. If you slip and go backwards, that's okay, but you have to move that marble temporarily back until you lose it again.

You will be amazed and empowered as you watch the marbles switch jars. Soon you will be displaying proud for all to see!

These magickal techniques will help you keep on track with your awareness, therefore positively reinforcing your eating and exercise—and making it a lot more fun!

MONEY MAGICK

෪෬

My Favorite Money Spell

Most everyone could use a little extra cash in their pocket. I learned this spell over twenty years ago. It is the simplest, easiest, and most effective spell imaginable. And . . . it has ALWAYS worked for me.

Before we get started, you will need to gather your simple supplies. What you need is a crisp, new dollar bill (or the nicest one you have). I much prefer REAL currency, but it can be play money if you prefer. Forewarning: It is illegal to burn money.** Get a pen, a fire safe bowl, a candle, and some incense.

Now, just as a reminder, the following are the most important components for successful spell casting:

- Passion fuels a successful spell; doubt can kill it.
- Have a clear goal.
- Rhyming is great! An old adage says that spells should rhyme. A rhymed spell has rhythm and joyfulness in it, it's easy to remember and repeat, and the repetition itself creates an altered, magickal consciousness.

First, create a "sacred" space. Say a prayer, call in the elements, play some music, whatever feels right. Be relaxed, yet focused (breathing can help, as well as a cleansing bath, shower, or meditation). Light the incense and candle. Call in YOUR divinity (God, universe, angels, guides, higher self, whatever words you use). I work elementally, so I am going to call in the air, fire, water, and earth elements.

Now, concentrate on the candle a couple minutes, watch the smoke of the incense, and think about all the material and monetary things you want to bring into your life. You can include things like zero balance on your credit card, a paid-in-full new car, money in the bank, etc. Really concentrate. I want you to literally see it, smell it, feel it, taste it in every cell of your body. Once you do, start passionately writing it on the dollar bill. You can write as much as you can cram in. (It's okay if it becomes illegible.) See yourself having these things NOW. When you have written everything you want on the bill (you can include pictures, signs, or sigils if you want), hold the dollar bill up. Wave it over the incense smoke three times. Keep your intention high.

Pass it over the candle three times and, on the third time, LIGHT THE DOLLAR BILL! My favorite time to do this is on a full moon and, for the burning part of the ritual, I do it outside under the light of the moon so I can watch the smoke drifting up to the heavens. You CAN do it whenever needed, of course, but if possible, it is best on the full moon itself—or during the period of the waxing moon.

Okay, back to the burning . . . this is where you have to really create the energy. Sway back and forth as it burns. Come up with a chant: "Money, money, money, come to me. Money, money, money now I see," or anything that suits your fancy. My favorite is a "maaa" chant, which I demonstrate on my money spell You-Tube video. Whichever method you are choosing, this is the part where you are building the energy up and up and up! When the last bit of the dollar burns (drop it into the fire-safe bowl to avoid burning your fingers), shoot all that energy and intention up into the universe. It is done! Say something like, "By the power of three times three, this spell bound round shall be," or just a great big "aho" or "amen" will do! Now, know that it has worked and go out and live into that reality. Check in with me when your spell starts working! Sometimes it's REALLY fast. Sometimes it takes a bit. But believe me: It has brought amazing abundance to tons of people I know for years now!

Now, follow those guidelines and go out and create some magick. The one real "rule" to remember is a spell is only used to control yourself, never another or nature. Do not do spell work on someone else's behalf without their permission. Before performing your spell, carefully think through all the possible repercussions to make certain that it does not have a manipulative component.

Always stay in integrity. Always work in the "light," and all will be well!

DRAGON MAGICK

In these crazy and chaotic times, I have been using a lot of Dragon magick. Dragons are magickal and powerful creatures. They are of Heaven and Earth, they are change makers and can cause real shift. Yes, I love fairies and angels and all other magickal and mystical creatures, but dragons have fire! The power of dragons can be a great influence not only in one's magickal working, but in day-to-day life as well.

Dragons are often called on as guardian spirits. They make for exceptional allies who can be called on in times of need, for protection or guidance. So if you would like to add a little dragon magick to your life, here's how.

Do take note: We are creating something real here, a real spirit that you create and call in. We are also creating something called a fetish or a golem. So take this seriously and do it with love and in light. A fetish or a golem is an inanimate object that you actually call life into, creating a living entity. This can become your assistant or working partner in life and in your magickal practice. We are calling in dragon energy into your fetish.

First, get a dragon. I use inexpensive little rubber or plastic dragons from the toy store, but you can use something fancier. You just need a vessel to house the spirit. You're going to need to come up with a name for your dragon, as well as its purpose—perhaps something like: "This dragon will help bring me love or help or health or happiness," "This dragon will get rid of roadblocks and fear," "This dragon will give me confidence," etc. I must forewarn you, though, that dragons are a little single-minded, so do not give it too many duties. The way to have multiple jobs, if needed, is to make your dragon your personal assistant. For example, you might direct in this way: "You are 'blank' the Magick Dragon. You are my personal assistant, and you will bring me opportunities, you will burn up and breathe away roadblocks, and you will keep me healthy and strong and confident!"

Since you are creating a real spirit, you also have to give it an end date, or it will be out there working for you for all of eternity. Say something like "until I don't need you or want you anymore." And then, when you say so, the spirit will dissipate and go back into the great nothingness and your vessel will again be just an empty toy.

Now that your dragon has a name and a job, you literally have to breathe life into it. Really concentrate, open up your spirit, put the dragon's mouth right up to yours, and give a deep, guttural breath into its mouth. Your breath is giving it life.

Care and feeding of your dragon: Keep your dragon on your altar or in a sacred or special place where you can see him or her every day. Remember to talk to it every day and keep it part of your life. Now, since it is a living creature, you do have to feed it. Well, give it drink, actually. Liquid is what I give my dragons. I hate to say it, but my dragons, and many other dragons, like alcohol. But, if you do not drink, or have an issue with drinking or alcohol, just feed your dragon apple juice or water or something else. Feed them regularly, and they will begin to let you know when they need more or want more. It will disappear. Refill as needed. If it does not disappear, throw it out as you would any offering and then give them new drink when needed. Some dragons get very mischievous and move around a little. Some dragons drink very fast, while others drink very slowly. You may have two dragons that drink the same thing at completely different paces, which sort of debunks the thought of simple evaporation. Have fun with your dragon. Respect your dragon, and you will have a good working partner in your life!

SOUND MAGICK

Next, I'd like to talk about the **Magick of Sound**. Cultures the world over use sound to attune to, invoke, and transform consciousness. Sound is a powerful tool because it is vibrational in nature, and we are vibrational beings.

Modern science shows us that all life is vibrational in nature. This is in line with age-old mystical thought of most cultures, which often allude to the vibrational nature of Creation. We have all experienced it, whether it be an "amen" at the end of a prayer or an "om" at the end of a yoga class.

From banging a loud gong to powerfully shift energy to the ringing of soft chimes to gently awaken the senses or spirits, I incorporate sound in many of my magickal workings. My favorite use of sound magick comes from the human voice, whether it be chanting and singing or the conscious use of specific sounds to evoke a specific outcome. This is called a "heka." Heka means the "art of sound," or alchemy of sound itself.

Here are some basic rules for Heka:
- Consonants are FORM: form that shapes.
- Vowels are FORCE: forces that ignite.

You can make up your own hekas from that! Try just doing vowel sounds—ahhh, ehhh, eeee, oooo, uuuuu—and see how invigorating it can be! Chanting vowel sounds is great before an important meeting or test where you need clarity and focus. Here are a few more meanings of sounds:

- U is a dragon vowel (nature into action). LOVE is the force/power.
- A is a vowel that brings birth/life.
- L is dragon in the land.
- Z is serpent—lightning strike between heaven and earth (divine wisdom).

Try using these sounds in a chant. Note how you feel, what you experience, what sight and senses open up, etc. Pretty cool, huh?! Powerful too!

Now, go out and make up your own power chants and sounds; I promise, it will open up a whole new magickal world for you! Remember, *Magick is EVERYWHERE!*

OUTDOOR MAGICK

I get out in nature every morning on my walk around Lake Hollywood. Getting outdoors is the perfect way to start or end your day—or you can even enjoy a quick walk on your lunch break. I find walking in nature (or even around the block) is a good time to do a little self-contemplation.

Gently ask yourself what needs revitalizing in your life. Hope? Passion? Health? Are you following your heart? It's like doing a little "light housekeeping" to look back and take stock of your day, your week, your year to date. Walking or strolling is a great way to contemplate what you have learned and look at where you want to go from here. It's a good time for sorting out unfinished business and choosing to free yourself from things that are hindering your progress, a good time to think about qualities you want to bring into your life and about the things that you are thankful for.

With all this thinking going on, you should now have a nice "to-do" list! Why not put it all into an outdoor ritual? Create a fun, simple ritual that encompasses your wishes and plans for the future, releases things that are not serving you, and gives thanks for what you have. You can make it up as you go. Get out in nature, hug a tree, and talk to the fairies. Tell your secrets and desires to an old oak. Release your fears and burdens into the wind.

Kick off your shoes and feel the earth beneath your feet as you pull up mother earth's energy through your entire body and give thanks. Pick up a rock and hold it up to your ear and listen to the wisdom it has to say to you. Send your prayers with a bird or butterfly in flight.

There are a million ways to connect to the magick all around you, especially outdoors and in nature. You are the creator of your life, so go out and make it happen. Commit and believe—and have fun with it. Remember, earth is sacred. Always respect nature and leave her natural, clean, and the way (or better than the way) you found her. There isn't a more beautiful church, temple, or ritual spot, in my opinion. Keep aware and find magick and divinity everywhere you go.

UNCROSSING MAGICK

ꪜ

My Favorite Uncrossing Spell

Every once and awhile, we need a good "uncross-ing" spell. Surprisingly, 99.9 percent of the time, it is NOT because someone put a real curse on you. Rather, you may just have a gathering of nega-tive energy, thoughts, and wishes that have swirled around and created an energy that you want to get rid of.

I do NOT do—or recommend—any kind of dark or manipulative magick. The "cost" is too high in the kickback and karma realms. So, when you do this spell, make sure you do NOT do this spell at a spe-cific person, just at the curse or dark energy itself. It will work on whomever and whatever it is sup-posed to.

You need a lemon, some sea salt, a knife, and a saucer. (You can use a black or dark saucer if you have one, but it's not required; any saucer will do!)

Cut lemon into four pieces while chanting three times:

"All spells against me congregate, within this lemon that's your fate. Sour spell to sour fruit, you must go there 'cuz that's your suit. Bound to this lemon ever more, each spell against me that's your store. All in this lemon now I see—and so it is, so mote it be."

Put the four slices on the saucer "pulp up." Keep chanting, feel it. Then sprinkle the salt all over the lemons. Sprinkle it thick, everywhere bottom and top, and chant:

"Uncrossed, uncrossed this salt for me. Breaks up attacking energy. Within this sour lemon bound, now kills all spells with salt and sound. As lemon dries in salt and air, I'm free from harm and all despair. Uncrossed, uncrossed and happy now you'll see— and as I will, so mote it be."

Keep chanting several times and feel it!

Now set the lemon aside. When it dries up, burn or bury it. If by chance it mildews, you need to do the spell again. This is very powerful, and it WORKS. ;o) Remember, magick is EVERYWHERE! For more info, please go to www.PattiNegri.com.

WHEN LOVED ONES PASS

ೋೋ

Dumb Supper

I usually get a double-take and an odd expression from people when one of their loved ones dies and I suggest they should do a Dumb Supper for them. True, the title is not the most flattering or what one would expect. However, in this case dumb does not mean stupid; it means silent. Some people are calling it a Silent Supper these days, but I'm going to stay with a double-take and odd expression.

You now may be asking yourself: "What is a Dumb Supper?" A Dumb Supper is a dinner you have for your beloved deceased to celebrate their passing. It is done forty days after their day of death. Forty days is the transition period between the worlds. It is true and honored in almost every culture, religion, and belief system around the world.

A Dumb Supper is done at or after the forty-day mark, and you will invite anyone you want. Have your favorite food or, better yet, have your deceased loved one's favorite food. It can be as simple or elaborate as you want, but it is a rewarding way to honor the dead and keep their memories alive.

Have dinner as usual, except do it backwards. Have the dessert first, then the main course, and then end with the soup or salad course. This shows the other side that it is for them, because things Beyond the Veil are reversed. Yes, you can be sad during the dinner, but mostly talk about things that you used to do together, laugh and talk with the person as if they are there with you, because they truly are!

Somewhere during the meal, spend a few minutes in silence. Your deceased loved one will communicate with each of you at the table to your own ability and comfort level. It may be a feeling or knowing that everything is okay. You may sense, feel, or even hear something. It is a very magickal few

minutes. Some people do the entire dinner in silence, but I have found over the years that complete silence is very hard in our modern world; people seem to get more satisfaction and closure from talking through most of it and just spending a small section in silence. Do whatever feels right to you.

At the end of the dinner (which is really the beginning since you are up to the soup or salad course), you say goodbye to your beloved in their fleshly form—that is the one thing you cannot have back. Whether you believe they go to heaven or they are reincarnated, or they just go on to the great consciousness of life (unless you want them as a zombie), their flesh is what you cannot have back. Let that go. Let them now be your spirit friend or loved one. This now can become a new and deeper relationship in that realm. Even your communication with them, if that is what you desire, will be stronger once it is now your spirit friend instead of your dead friend. It is a beautiful, healing, cathartic, and even fun experience. It is one of my favorite rituals. Remember it next time a loved one passes to the other side.

KEEPING CALM IN THE STORM

೧೨೦

No matter what your spiritual belief system or political views, it is so obvious we are living in crazy times.

I have chosen to not get political here, but I will confess I am not happy with the current state of things. The world is shifting. Energy is chaotic and overwhelming. People are frightened, angry, uncertain, confused—or all of the above! So I thought I would give a few simple "survival" tips to help get you through this transition with a little bit of grace and ease.

One: Take time for yourself. No one will give you the time; you must MAKE it, whether you choose to get up ten minutes earlier, stay up later, or do a little less social media or TV time. We all need extra grounding and balance right now to help us focus. Meditate, pray, take a walk in nature, paint, draw, sing, whatever works for you, but make it a daily habit. I promise, a tiny little shift will make a BIG difference in how you get through the rest of the day.

Two: Take a simple white bath! There is nothing more magickal and cleansing than a simple white bath. As explained earlier, I like to add a little salt for cleansing, a little sugar for sweetness, and some milk for nurturing. You may feel a little bit like a bowl of cereal, but the magickal attributes in each of these ingredients really will make you feel like a million bucks! Just use a half cup to a cup of each, and you can rinse off afterwards! If you don't have access to a bathtub, pour the ingredients on you in the shower. Have fun with it!

Three: Take care of yourself. Eat a little better, exercise a little more, make sure you get enough sleep. Again, no one else will do it for you—and it WILL make a difference! (*Try adding my Dream School technique from the June 2016 newsletter on my website, http://bit.ly/DreamSchoolTechnique. As well as spiritual development, the water will help you sleep!*)

Four: Get outside and look up at the sky! It will give you a bit of perspective on how big the universe is. Let it inspire you.

Five: Consciously create your reality. Decide things DO matter—from what color outfit you choose to wear that day, to your thoughts, words, and actions. Stand up for what you believe in. Think for yourself. You CAN make a difference. You DO make a difference.

Six: Remember to breathe.

SPECTROPHILIA (GHOST SEX!)

✷

I am considered an expert in spectrophilia, which is human and spirit intimacy. It has been written about through all of time, and usually has a bad rap to the negative sides—as in incubus and succubus, where demons come down and take mortals to their liking. But in my experience with clients, there is the good side of that as well, with deceased spouses and loved ones who come back to comfort. It is funny that so many think that this is taboo or wrong, since sex is such a big part of our human experience. Why would we think it would not carry over?

If you believe in spirits, and you believe Grandma can come and stand at the end of your bed and comfort you, why wouldn't you believe your deceased spouse can come and do the same in a more intimate way? Again, thought-provoking, but something many people seem to experience in a positive and loving way. I do believe spirits can still experience intimacy. It is part of who we are, our energetic experience. If we have moved into the world of spirit, maybe just everything is love! :-) That's the way I like to think about it anyway.

MY GHOST ADVENTURES

CHASING SPIRITS WITH ZAK BAGANS AND
THE BOYS OF *GHOST ADVENTURES!*

I am lucky and honored to be brought in regularly on the hit TV show *Ghost Adventures!* It is the number one paranormal show in the world, now entering its tenth year and sixteenth season on the Travel Channel. The host, star, and producer, Zak Bagans, has called me in on several episodes as a psychic and medium and often to conduct one of my signatures séances. It is always quite the adventure, partially because I never know what I am getting into (I absolutely love that!). *Ghost Adventures* is extraordinarily good about authenticity. They go to great lengths to make sure everything is real, in the moment, and not set up or planned.

I have been to some of the most haunted sites in the world with them! I have helped them talk to spirits in the "Haunted Hollywood" episode, conducted a séance at the infamous and scary Black Dahlia House, led them to my most haunted venue in Reseda House of Evil, and another infamous murder house in Chatsworth. I have even held my first-ever séance with a VERY haunted doll named Peggy in "Deadly Possessions." I have communed with dead rock stars in the Infamous "Alley" episode. I was brought in for the big Halloween special in 2017 and the four-hour LIVE Halloween special in 2018. I am forever grateful for the opportunities and adventures Zak Bagans and his Ghost Adventures bring me!

Here is a fun little "day-in-the-life" moment from my "Deadly Possessions" episode:

As usual, I had no idea what I was getting into. All I knew was that I had received a phone call from a rather anxious Zak, saying he needed me to fly to Las Vegas to do a séance with a haunted doll. He apparently knew that I was also a "doll person" and collector. For some reason, this particular doll seemed to have extra importance and urgency to him.

When I arrived in Las Vegas and was taken to my hotel, immediately strange things started happening. My brand-new cell phone went completely haywire. My brand-new tablet started mimicking it and also started doing strange and never-before-seen oddities. My first reaction was "technical aggravation" over "some spirit doesn't want me here." But, knowing my phone was my communication lifeline when filming (when to be ready to be picked up to go to set, etc.), I knew I had to deal with it. So I proceeded to spend over four hours on the phone with my cell provider's technical department, going all the way to their top expert technicians and leaving them all dumbfounded one by one—so much so that they literally overnighted me a new phone (almost unheard of with my provider!). As the night wore on, I started realizing this was not just a bad cell phone; something far larger was at play here.

I started sensing an ominous spirit hanging over me, a spirit that really didn't want me here. And I was not in a dark, scary haunted house, but far from it. I was in an ultra-modern luxury high rise hotel on the Vegas strip—not the typical setting for the now-overwhelming darkness encompassing me. I decided to watch some TV. Nope, spirit had other plans. I would turn on the TV in the living room and then something would turn it off and turn on the TV in the bedroom or bathroom.

Fine, got it. I'll take a shower and go to bed. Shenanigans continued, even with my shower water turning itself back on as I stepped out to dry. Now I was getting VERY excited as to what kind of doll I was going to meet the next day.

The next morning, I was picked up and taken to Zak Bagans' newly created Haunted Museum, a sprawling 1930s era Tudor revival cottage. It was not what you expect for find in downtown Vegas, but was perfectly befitting Zak, his museum, and haunted treasures! Tensions were already high. Zak excitedly showed me around some of his wonderful new displays, but was very careful NOT to tell me anything about the doll or just what we were doing, until we were actually on camera and filming.

I was sequestered in a room with a mix of haunted items, paintings, cameras, filming equipment, and a few curious spirits. My excitement was piqued by the time I was led in to film my first segment with Zak. There on camera he told me a tiny bit about Peggy the Haunted Doll, the ill effects she had on people, and how he was truly concerned, even for viewers once the show went to air.

The thickness of the energy had reached an all-time high by the time we went into the séance room and I first met the doll's owner, Jayne Harris, one of the doll's victims, Katrin—and, of course, Peggy the Haunted Doll. The focus of the séance was Katrin releasing the negative power that Peggy had over her, as her fear fed it. Katrin was a rock star. She even let us leave her alone in the room with the doll for a few minutes. She faced her fears and won!

During the séance, I tuned in to a beautiful female spirit inside Peggy. She was obviously not the entity giving people literal heart attacks and making them sick; that was something darker, deeper, and more hidden. I got glimpses of this darker spirit through-out the rest of the day. That is the spirit that sent flies to attack Zak and caused true physical harm to Katrin and so many others.

As all this was going on, I was also very aware of the doll's owner Jayne and her energy, strength, psychic awareness, and power. I was glad. She is the perfect guardian for Peggy the Haunted Doll. The girl spirit within Peggy is a bright light. The darker, more hid-den spirit is just the opposite. Jayne has quite an amazing and complicated task and responsibility with this most amazing of dolls!

One of my favorite things about working with the *Ghost Adventure* crew is their total commitment to what they are doing. There is a good reason the show is such a long-running hit. They put 100 percent into every investigation, long nights in the most inconve-nient and haunted locations around the world—and yet every new adventure is as exciting and new as the first one. I am a lucky girl indeed to get to share some of these amazing and otherworldly experiences!

SOME OF MY EXPERIENCES

⚬⚬

To me, everything is energy! Spirits are energy. Spirits and entities appear in several ways to me and often to participants in my séances, depending both on their comfort level and acceptance—as well as the entities' ability or type. Often I get light anomalies that enter and fly around the room. That seems to be an easy way for them to show their presence. Sometimes it comes as shadows, mists, scents, changes in temperature, a slight touch, or full-on visions of beings.

Rarely is a séance like you see in the movies; it's a bit more subtle. Often you see the beings in the corner of your eye, like seeing a shadow or light pass by, or a shadowy form of a person where you can make out certain details. I have also had some very big and obvious experiences as well, things that were noticeable enough to be seen on film.

A couple years ago I was conducting a séance for a group of young college students. I thought it was going to be a small group of curious kids, but it turned out to be a full classroom of kids—including their professors from the philosophy and psychology departments. I felt a bit "duped," like it was a big gathering to "disprove the crazy lady." But in reality, the energy in the room was SO amazing. (Young people have incredible energy; when directed correctly, it is awesome!) The lights/entities came into the room so brightly and were flying around back and forth and up and down, and we had literally forty people seeing and experiencing the whole thing. It sounded like we were riding a roller coaster with the oohs and aahs, and it looked like everyone was watching an amazing tennis match, with heads in unison going left then right then left again! Then, I was flooded with information for several of the people there—personal, important messages for many of them. Jaws dropped. This was not the experience they were expecting! Plus this all took place on their turf. I had never stepped foot in the location before, or met a single person there, so they knew there could be no trickery involved.

Once I was doing a séance at a very haunted old home in the Hollywood Hills. The former tenants included silent film star Mary Astor, The Rolling Stones, the Mamas & the Papas and, most recently, Marilyn Manson. The house had a dark, tangled energy and literally drew chaotic, creative people to it. I knew that house would never be happy with a "normal" family living there. I could also feel that there was an angry spirit present who was not happy we were there. We had two film crews shooting the séance for two different projects, one of which was a documentary about the house.

The séance participants were the current tenants and their friends and neighbors. I think there were about a dozen people total. I explained to everyone how I worked, set up the space, and established protections. I asked the participants to keep an open mind, to take it seriously, and to be respectful of what we were doing and any spirits who may appear.

We were starting to get some real insights and finding out some dark information about things that had happened in the house in the 1920s. One of the participants started getting a little "smart alecky" and making wisecracks. Things started happening immediately. The French doors flew open on their own accord. The speakers, which were not even plugged in or turned on, started making static or white noise on and off, and the energy was building and building so that everyone could feel it. One more wisecrack from the guy and, all of a sudden, my cameraman—who was directly across from him and shooting in his direction—burst into flames! The flames started shooting up his back in a V shape, almost like angel wings of fire. They burned his shirt right off like it was synthetic, but it was all cotton. Everyone was screaming and jumping up from the table. The medic in me came out and I yelled, "Drop and roll," and before we knew it, the whole thing was over.

Blisters started forming on his lower back by the end of the evening, but he said he was okay. We decided to continue the séance. I laid down a LOT more protection, called in more wards, and got serious with the participants about being respectful (they now had no problem obeying). We had one more glass literally fly out of a cupboard after filming, but I was able to calm the angry spirit.

When I saw the cameraman's scar a few weeks later, it had taken the exact shape of a dragon with big teeth, winged ears, and body narrowing down into a serpent. It was pretty amazing. I believe it was dragon energy that came in to protect him—and now he had quite the keepsake. It all turned out well, and we got some great footage, but it could've had a disastrous ending.

My advice to anyone working in this realm is most importantly: RESPECT the paranormal and its power! You have to know what you are doing. This is not a game. Study, learn, and make sure you are trained and well-versed in paranormal principles and psychic protection methods. Whatever cosmology or modality you are working in, really know it! Be very clear as to who or what you are inviting in, and make sure that anyone with you takes it just as seriously and follows your rules and guidelines. Always work in the light. Be clear to only invite in friendly, benevolent, helpful spirits and entities, and be firm that no others are allowed into your sacred space. Please be aware that the world you create is the world you have to live in; so if you want to open up the veil and live in a world with ghosts and spirits, make sure they are friendly ones!

ON LOCATION FILMING "RESEDA HOUSE OF EVIL"

AARON GOODWIN, BILLY TOLLEY, ME, ZAK BAGANS,
HAUNTED HOMEOWNER DEVON KLYNE, JAY WASLEY

PEGGY THE HAUNTED DOLL SÉANCE AT ZAK'S
HAUNTED MUSEUM IN LAS VEGAS

SPIRIT RESIDUE ON KATRIN'S CHAIR RIGHT AFTER
THE PEGGY THE HAUNTED DOLL SÉANCE

ABOUT THE AUTHOR

Patti is a psychic-medium and "good" witch. She was voted world's number one psychic, medium, trance medium, tarot reader, witch/magickal practitioner, crystal & stone energy healer and life coach this year in an international competition by Times Square Press. In addition, she also won number one Intuitive Entertainer Occult Personality of the year and number one Influential Woman in Business. She has recently graced six magazine covers, including American Psychic & Medium, Art, UFO and

Supernatural, Parapsychology and Mind Power, 4th Dimension, and Stars Illustrated and has contributed or been a part of over twenty books, several of which are Amazon bestsellers.

Patti has been able to communicate with the spirit world since she was a toddler and consciously conducted her first séance at age eight. Since then, she has conducted séances, clearings, and sessions on radio, film, TV, and in living rooms across America.

Patti enjoys working her magick on television. She has just completed her seventh episode of *Ghost Adventures* and their spinoff *Deadly Possessions* on the Travel Channel, cleared spaces on Jeff Lewis's *Flipping Out*, done some magickal cooking on *Master Chef* with Gordon Ramsey, conjured up a few "dead celebrities" on *Private Chefs of Beverly Hills, Beverly Hills Pawn* and several episodes of *Pit Boss* and two episodes of *Bad Girls Club*. Patti was brought in as a paranormal expert on *Ghostly Lovers, Candidly Nicole, Mansion Hunters, Beverly Hills Pawn,* and dozens more. She has even gotten into the home makeover world on *Mobile Home Disaster*. In addition to being a host of several of her own radio shows on Blogtalk Radio, Patti has been heard on national syndicated radio with *Adam Corolla, Jason Ellis,* and *Mancow Muller.*

As a performer, Patti has enjoyed numerous stage, film, and television roles, and has had the honor of working with Martin Sheen, Burt Reynolds, Jon Voight, John C. Riley, Ernie Hudson, Josh Duhamel, Chevy Chase, and Sylvester Stallone, to name a few. She has danced with Gregory Hines, choreographed for David Hasselhoff, and entertained celebrities on scavenger hunts and toga mysteries across the Greek Islands. As a producer, Patti owns Brain Brew Entertainment, a theatrical production company that specializes in live entertainment.

Patti's working style is magickal, loving, and upbeat, which creates a positive, safe, and fun environment for you to learn, grow, and heal. She has been practicing natural magick her entire life. Her specialty is in adjusting energy and flow—in people, spaces, situations, most anything. She works organically by creating spells and rituals that arrange natural elements to the rhythms and cycles of the universe to bring about healing, change our lives for the better, and create balance.

Patti is available for corporate events and parties for one-on-one readings, group gallery style readings. She is also available for workshops, teaching, motivational and speaking engagements, as well as media, television, and radio. Patti is based in Los Angeles, but travels worldwide in service to spiritual adventures.

Sessions can include: tarot, intuitive reading, channeling, journey work, coaching, empowerment training, past life work, energy balancing, spell working, and whatever is needed to best serve your needs. Patti also offers training internationally in psychic development, magickal working, and self-empowerment. Sessions and training can be live, phone, or Skype.

Call or email for more information and pricing for séances, house blessings, speaking and teaching engagements, etc.

Website:
www.pattinegri.com

Email:
patti@pattinegri.com

Twitter:

twitter.com/PattiNegri

Facebook:

facebook.com/PattiNegriPsychicMedium

Patti is honored to be President and Chief Examiner of the American Federation of Certified Psychics and Mediums.

Made in the USA
Monee, IL
19 January 2023

25696920R00069